By James Edward

Character illustrations by Jon Stuart

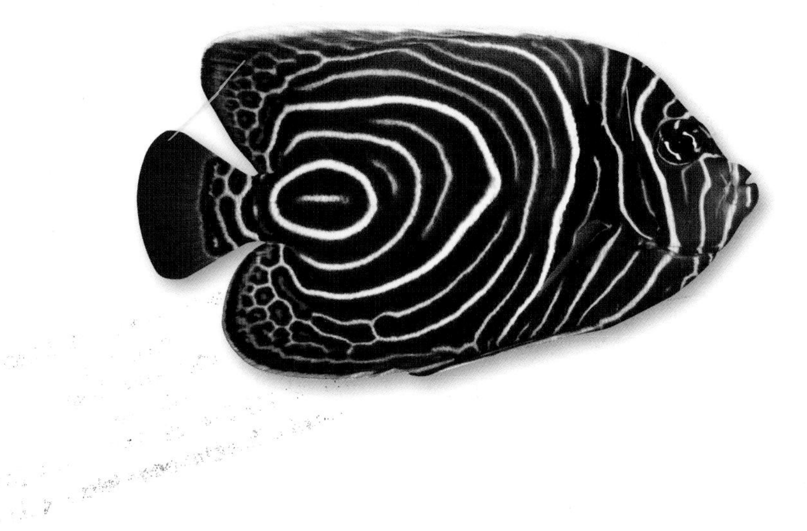

READ

We are going to have a look deep down under the sea.

We are going on an amazing diving adventure to the biggest coral reef in the world.

It is called the Great Barrier Reef, and it lies off the coast of Australia.

We will meet some of the colourful creatures that live there.

TALK

- Talk with children about where Australia is, and find it together on a globe or map. Point out the Great Barrier Reef on the east coast.

ACTIVITY

- Point to the word *shark* and ask children to sound-talk it (i.e. shark becomes sh-ar-k).
- Then ask children to blend the sounds together and say the word (i.e. sh-ar-k becomes shark).

Tip

See the inside back cover for more guidance on sounds.

READ

This is a coral reef. It lies under the sea and is home to thousands of plants and animals.

You can see some of the animals in this picture.

You can see fish, a starfish and an eel.

TALK

- Ask children what different colours they can see on the sea creatures.

ACTIVITY

- Ask children to identify the common sounds in the words *curling* and *turning*. (/ur/, /i/, /ng/)
- **Have some fun!** Paint, draw or use coloured tissue paper or foil to make a picture or collage of life under the sea. Remember to use bright colours.

I can see an eel curling and turning.

starfish

eel

READ

A coral reef looks like a big rock, but it is actually a living thing.

It is built from millions of tiny sea creatures called coral polyps. When the polyps die, they leave behind a skeleton. Over thousands of years, the skeletons become reefs.

There are many different types of coral and they come in lots of different colours and shapes. This is what gives a coral reef its amazing beauty.

TALK

- Look at the picture, and talk with children about the different shapes they can see (e.g. round, flat, spiky, frilly).

ACTIVITY

- Read the following sentence and ask children to say the missing word: *The coral is sharp. If Max is not careful, his wetsuit will get …* (clue: it rhymes with *born*). (torn)
- Ask children to write the word *torn*. Children could use magnetic letters, a whiteboard or a pencil and paper to write.

a coral reef

The reef is hard and sharp.

brain coral

READ

Fish swim in and out of the coral reef. They swim in big groups called shoals.

Just like the coral reef, the fish come in lots of different colours and sizes.

The fish can be difficult to spot against the colourful coral.

TALK

- A group of fish is called a shoal. Talk with children about the names for other groups of animals. Can they think of any others (e.g. a herd of cows, a flock of sheep)?

ACTIVITY

- Ask the children to count how many letters are in the words *shoal* (5) and *bright* (6).
- Ask children to sound-talk the words (e.g. shoal becomes sh-oa-l).
- Then ask children to blend the sounds and say the words (e.g. sh-oa-l becomes shoal).

Look at that big shoal of fish!

This reef is bright pink!

READ

Clownfish are brightly-coloured fish that live amongst the tentacles of sea anemones.

The beautiful sea anemone looks like a plant, but it is an animal. It uses its stinging tentacles to catch fish.

The clownfish has a special slimy coat that protects it from the anemone's tentacles.

TALK

- Ask children if they have read any stories or watched any films about fish or the sea. Can they remember what happened?

ACTIVITY

- Read out the following sentence to children: *The fish will not get hurt.*
- Use a pen and paper to write the word *hurt*. Ask children to put sound buttons under the word (i.e. **h ur t**) and then blend sounds to read the word.

This animal can sting.

The fish cannot feel the sting.

READ

Sharks live near the coral reef, too. They hunt around the reef for fish.

People are scared of sharks, but reef sharks do not attack humans.

Reef sharks are in danger because too many of them have been caught by fishermen. There are not many left, and they might die out.

reef shark

TALK

- Tell children some more facts about sharks:
  - The biggest shark is the whale shark. It can grow up to fifteen metres in length.
  - Great white sharks can go up to three months without eating.
  - The hammerhead shark has a head shaped like a hammer.

ACTIVITY

- **Have some fun!** Use the Internet to find pictures of a whale shark, great white shark and hammerhead shark.

The shark is
looking for food.

READ

This is a stingray.

It is a large flat creature that lurks on the seafloor looking for crabs and fish.

Be careful not to step on one. Stingrays have poisonous spikes, called barbs, on their tails.

Don't worry. They will not attack unless they feel they are in danger or get stepped on.

Look at its sharp tail!

tail

TALK

- Ask children if they can think of anything else in the sea that might sting them (e.g. jellyfish, urchin).

ACTIVITY

- Read out the following sentence to children and ask them to say the missing word: *Some boats have a big white …* (clue: it rhymes with *tail*). (sail)
- Ask children to write the word *sail*.

barb

The barb on its tail can sting.

READ

We have been looking at life on the Great Barrier Reef.

Look at all the animals and fish that we met ...

ACTIVITY

- **Have some fun!** Use a book or look on the Internet to find out how fish breathe under water.